AIRPLANE

BY ALEX SUMMERS

R urke
Educational Media
rourkeeducationalmedia.com

Scan for Related Titles
and Teacher Resources

Before & After Reading Activities

Teaching Focus:
Concepts of Print: Have students find capital letters and punctuation in a sentence. Ask students to explain the purpose for using them in a sentence.

Before Reading:

Building Academic Vocabulary and Background Knowledge

Before reading a book, it is important to set the stage for your child or student by using pre-reading strategies. This will help them develop their vocabulary, increase their reading comprehension, and make connections across the curriculum.

1. Read the title and look at the cover. *Let's make predictions about what this book will be about.*
2. Take a picture walk by talking about the pictures/photographs in the book. Implant the vocabulary as you take the picture walk. Be sure to talk about the text features such as headings, the Table of Contents, glossary, bolded words, captions, charts/diagrams, or Index.
3. Have students read the first page of text with you then have students read the remaining text.
4. Strategy Talk – use to assist students while reading.
   - Get your mouth ready
   - Look at the picture
   - Think…does it make sense
   - Think…does it look right
   - Think…does it sound right
   - Chunk it – by looking for a part you know
5. Read it again.

Content Area Vocabulary
Use glossary words in a sentence.

clouds
engines
pilot
wings

After Reading:

Comprehension and Extension Activity

After reading the book, work on the following questions with your child or students in order to check their level of reading comprehension and content mastery.

1. *What are some things people do while they are riding an airplane? (Summarize)*
2. *What kind of things can you see on an airplane? (Asking Questions)*
3. *If you could take an airplane somewhere, where would you go? (Text to self connection)*
4. *Who flies the airplane and where does he/she sit? (Asking Questions)*

Extension Activity

Make Your Own Airplane! Have an adult help you follow the instructions on www.foldnfly.com to fold your own paper airplane. Throw it through the air to see if it can fly. How far did it go?

I know. I will take an
airplane. It is REALLY big.

The **pilot** flies the plane.
He sits in the cockpit.

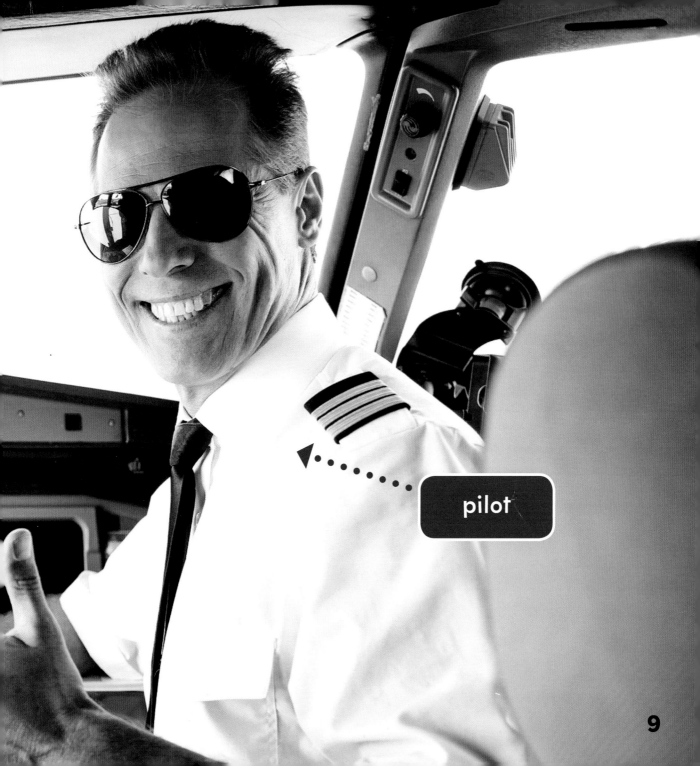

pilot

The airplane has two **wings**.
They help the plane fly.

wing

I fasten my seat belt. An attendant explains the safety rules.

attendant

13

Take Off!

The **engines** make a loud sound. My tummy tickles when we take off.

engine

I can see the **clouds**.
We fly right through them.

I watch a movie. I get a drink and snack.

How We Land

The pilot puts down the wheels. We land on a runway.

wheels

Flying is fun!

Picture Glossary

 **clouds** (klouds): A mass of condensed water vapor floating in the sky.

 **engines** (EN-jins): Machines that make something move by using energy.

 **pilot** (PILOT): A person who flies an airplane.

 **wings** (wings): Structures that stick out the side of an airplane that help it fly.

Index

Websites to Visit

www.sciencekids.co.nz/sciencefacts/vehicles/airplanes.html

www.educationworld.com

www.sciencekids.co.nz/lessonplans/flight.html

About the Author

Alex Summers enjoys all forms of transportation. Especially if they are taking her to places she has never been or seen before. She loves to travel, read, write, and dream about all the places she will visit someday!

Meet The Author!
www.meetREMauthors.com

Library of Congress PCN Data

Airplane / Alex Summers
(Transportation and Me!)
ISBN 978-1-68342-162-7(hard cover)
ISBN 978-1-68342-204-4 (soft cover)
ISBN 978-1-68342-231-0 (e-Book)
Library of Congress Control Number: 2016956591

Rourke Educational Media
Printed in the United States of America,
North Mankato, Minnesota

Also Available as:

www.rourkeeducationalmedia.com

Edited by: Keli Sipperley
Cover design by: Tara Raymo
Interior design by: Rhea Magaro-Wallace
Photo Credits: Cover, title page, page 11 © Chinnasorn Pangchareon; page 5, 7, 22 © suzieleaky; page 5 © Talaj, kamski, JackF, Gugurat; page 7 © Tezcankemal; page 8 © g-stockstudio; page 12 © TShooterTShooter; page 16 © MINGUA ZHANG; page 22 © Senohrabek